Snake

Armadillo

Monkey

Scorpion

Jaguar

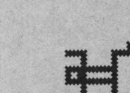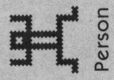

Duck

Person

Iguana

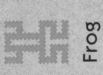

Frog

Bat

Count with me

1 to 10

Ana Palmero Cáceres

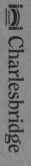 Charlesbridge

one

2
two
snakes

three
armadillos

four
monkeys
47

the

5

scorpions
five

six ducks

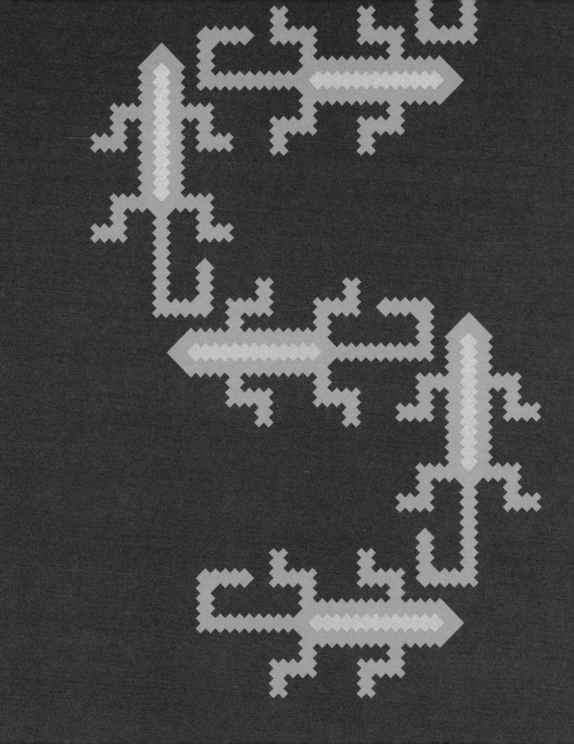

seven

iguanas

eight

bats

nine frogs

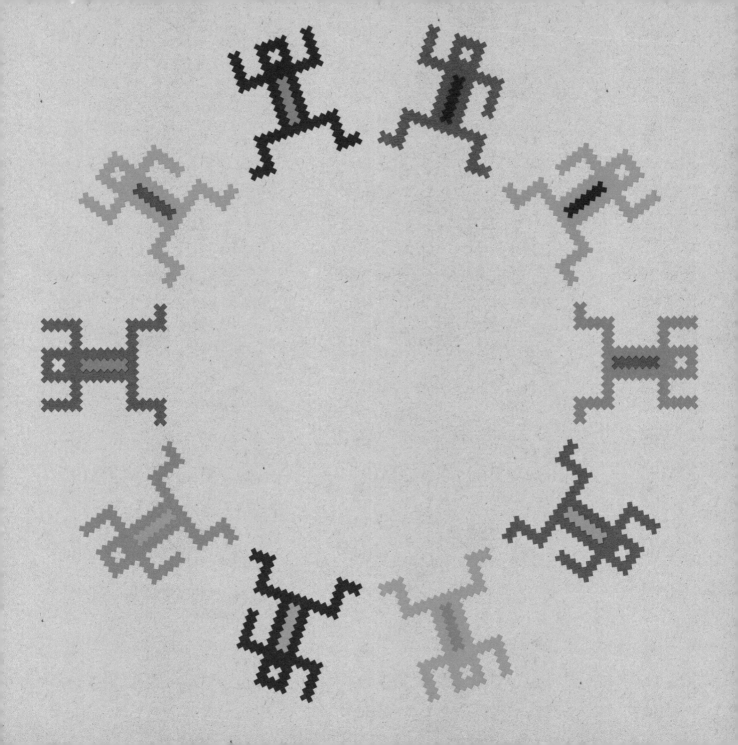

ten
people

one	two	three	four	five
1	2	3	4	5
jaguar	snakes	armadillos	monkeys	scorpions

six 6 ducks

seven 7 iguanas

eight 8 bats

nine 9 frogs

ten 10 people

In this book, I borrowed ideas from the baskets of the Ye'kuana people who live in southern Venezuela along the Orinoco River. Designs vary depending on each weaver, but all have complex geometric patterns.

The first time I saw wapas, I knew I loved the shapes on the baskets. Some woven designs represent sacred animals, like the snake, monkey, or frog. In other cases, abstract designs are used.

A **wuwa** is an hourglass-shaped basket. It is used for decoration and to store food.

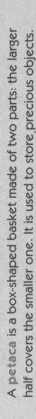

A **petaca** is a box-shaped basket made of two parts: the larger half covers the smaller one. It is used to store precious objects.

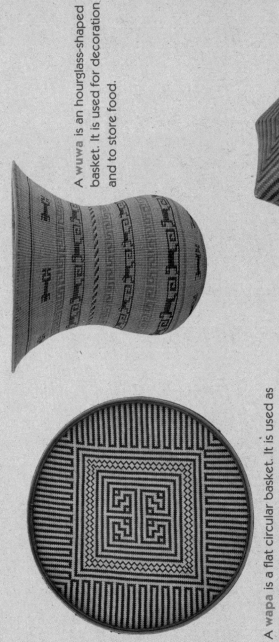

A **wapa** is a flat circular basket. It is used as a sieve to collect yuca (a plant used to make casabe, a kind of bread) and as a container for objects.

There is no standard way to write words from the Ye'kuana language.

The writing used by anthropologists and linguists varies.

The translations below represent one version of words for the numbers and animals in this book.

Jaguar	Mado	1	Toni
Snake	Ocoyu	2	Akü
Armadillo	Kajau	3	Aaduawö
Monkey	Yadaakadu	4	Aaköichea
Scorpion	Münötö	5	Ijaatodea
Duck	Jaatu	6	Toni amöjaato
Iguana	Yamanadi	7	Akü amöjaato
Bat	Dede	8	Aduawö amöjaato
Frog	Kütto	9	Aköichea amöjaato
Person	So'to	10	Amojadö

To the weavers of the Amazonia—A. P. C.

2019 First US edition

Translation copyright © 2019 by Charlesbridge Publishing, Inc.

Translated by Carlos E. Calvo.

Published by Charlesbridge
85 Main Street
Watertown, MA 02472
(617) 926-0329
www.charlesbridge.com

First published in Spanish as *Cuéntame del 1 al 10.*
© Ana Palmero Cáceres;
© Edicions Ekaré, Caracas, Venezuela.
www.ekare.com

Acknowledgments: Rafael Santana, Ronny Vélasquez, Alessandra Caputo, and Tarek Mileton

Library of Congress Cataloging-in-Publication Data

Names: Palmero Cáceres, Ana, author, illustrator.

Title: Count with me : 1 to 10 / Ana Palmero Cáceres.

Other titles: Cuéntame del 1 al 10. English

Description: First US edition. | Watertown, MA : Charlesbridge, 2018. | "First published in Spanish as *Cuéntame del 1 al 10* by Edicions Ekaré."

Identifiers: LCCN 2017056278 |

ISBN 9781580898928 (reinforced for library use) |

ISBN 9781632897619 (ebook pdf) | ISBN 9781632897602 (ebook)

Subjects: LCSH: Counting—Juvenile literature. | Yecuana baskets—Juvenile literature. | Yecuana Indians—Juvenile literature. | Yecuana literature.

Classification: LCC QA113 .P3461813 2018 | DDC 513.2—dc23

LC record available at https://lccn.loc.gov/2017056278

Printed in China
(hc) 10 9 8 7 6 5 4 3 2 1

Display type set in Insignia by Linotype
Text type set in ITC Kabel by Adobe
Printed by 1010 Printing International Limited in Huizhou, Guangdong, China
Production supervision by Brian G. Walker
Designed by Sarah Richards Taylor